# Keto Air Fryer for Beginners

5-Ingredient Affordable, Quick & Healthy Budget Friendly Recipes | Heal Your Body & Help You Lose Weight

Karen Tater

## Table of contents

# Introduction

There is a misconception that if you want to walk the healthy path, you have to give up fried and delicious foods!

The Cosori Air Fryer is actually here to change that perspective and help you understand that it is actually possible to stay healthy, while consuming fried foods at the same time!

Trust me, I am not misleading you here! The technology of an Air Fryer is just that much fascinating.

This awesome appliance works by frying the meals by pushing in extremely hot Air and frying up the meals with no hassle. And the best part? Since the food are cooked by air and requires no direct contact with heat source, therefore it requires almost none to no amount of oil!

It has a built-in fan that circulates hot air around the food and cooks it to perfection, soft on the inside and crispy crunchy on the outside.

And the best part? Using this appliance, you will be able to follow your Keto Diet with no effort at all! Since the Air Fryer allows rapid cooking, even if you are a busy individual, the Air Fryer will allow you to prepare Air Fried Keto meals with ease.

# Chapter 1: Understanding Keto Diet

## What is Ketogenic Diet

In the simplest of terms, the Ketogenic Diet is a form of diet that encourages a diet regime that boasts a dietary routine that asks you to follow a low-carb food plan that is high in fact and moderately packed with protein.

That being said, the primary target of the program is to trim down your daily carb intake so that you can influence your body to enter a state known as "Ketosis'.

Once you are able to do that, your body will basically turn into a fat burning machine!

But keep in mind, that there is a certain macro requirement that you should know about while following a Keto Diet, in short:

- Take 15-30% calories from your protein
- Take 5-10% calories from carbs
- Take 60-75% of calories from fat

However, this might vary from one person to the next, so these are not set in stones.

## The Process of Ketosis

As you can see, the main purpose of Ketogenic Diet is to push your body into "Ketosis", so it is only fair that we dig a little deeper in this concept and explore what does this actually mean.

In the simplest terms, Ketosis is basically a naturally occurring state of the body that is initiated when the body experiences a shortage of carbohydrates. During Ketosis, the body starts to use and burn more fat in order to produce the energy required for day to day tasks.

Ketosis and Ketogenic Diet are linked to a wide number of different health benefits! Including rapid weight loss and protection against various diseases such as Cancer or Type-1 Diabetes.

The word "Keto" is derived from a type of molecule known as "Ketones" that act as small fuel molecules in the body as an alternative to carbohydrates. These are produced from fat that we consume and are produced whenever our body notices a shortage of glucose.

So, whenever you are diminishing carbohydrates from your body and pushing it to Ketosis, fat starts to convert to Ketones in the liver, which later on enters your bloodstream.

These are then used to fuel the different cells of your body.

Since fat is present in large quantities in your body, Ketosis significantly accelerates the fat burning process while keeping your energy packed all throughout the day.

## Advantages of Ketogenic Diet

The Keto Program is a very carefully planned program that allows your body to experience a whole lot of amazing health benefits in the long run. Just some of the awesome ones are given below:

- Properly following the Keto Program will prevent blockades from occurring in your artery by lowering down the amount of bad cholesterol that you consume

- Since your body will be burning more and more fat, you will never feel lethargic and your body will stay energized throughout the day
- Since the amount of bad cholesterol will go down in your body, you will develop a greater immunity towards Type-2 Diabetes
- The program will allow you to control your hunger and you won't feel as much hungry anymore
- This is a lesser known fact, but the Keto diet also helps to significantly improve the condition of your skin and help prevent inflammation

But I guess you are more interested in knowing how a Ketogenic Diet can trim down your big right? Well...

- Since the Keto Diet will start to burn fat as the primary source of energy, it will vastly accelerate the rate at which your body will trim down fat
- The Ketogenic Diet has been designed to ensure that your body gets a very good amount of protein, the above average intake of protein will contribute to trimming down your body fat as well
- Once you are restricting your body from eating more carbs rich food, naturally your daily calorie intake will see a drastic cut as well, which will further help to trim your fat
- Once your body goes into Keto mode, Gluconeogenesis will start activate itself, which will further contribute to your weight losing journey
- And last but not the least, the carefully designed Ketogenic program will help you to keep your appetite under control. This basically means that asides from being able to trim down your weight, you will also be able to control your portions, making sure that you don't accidentally eat up unwanted calories or carbs.

So, as you can see, the diet won't only help you to trim down your weight, it will keep you healthy as well!

## Why Keto is Suitable for Americans

Recent studies have shown that Americans, especially the young ones and individuals who are extremely busy and are unable to produce to their own meal at home, tend to overly rely on consuming fast foods and other types of junk foods.

These types are of food are usually full of fat, meat and contain almost no nutritional values accompanying them. Not to mention, junk foods such as burgers contain a buck load of cheese!

We completely understand that all of a sudden changing your diet and altering your complete food regime can be difficult to many individuals.

However, when considering the daily lifestyle of Americans, making a shift to the Ketogenic diet isn't that hard actually!

As you already know, at its core the Ketogenic Diet encourages an individual to let go of Carbohydrates while focusing more on foods that are low in carb and rich in fat and protein contents.

So, generally you will have to consume cheese, nuts, fish, butter, sausage, meat, egg etc.

These items are not that much different from average American eats on a daily basis! The difference is that, they don't know the right balance, and they use ingredients that are high in carbs.

Therefore, if you are an American, making very simple changes to your diet should prepare you for the Ketogenic and start following it effortlessly.

## Amazing tips for your Keto Diet

While keeping your carb count under wrap will help stay on the right track, the following tips should help you improve the effectiveness of your program even further!

- Try to get yourself a nice carb counter to keep track of your daily intake.
- Get rid of all the high-carb produces and meals from your cup board.
- Restock your pantry using only suitable low carb ingredients.
- Makeup and follow a strict meal plan
- Slowly and steadily give up your hold habits and accept the new ones that will compliment your Keto Diet
- Always remember to keep a good amount of water close to you and be prepared to stay hydrated always.
- Once you have decided that you are going to jump into a Ketogenic Diet, one thing which you might find interesting to follow is a technique known as "Intermittent fasting".
  This basically tells you that you should start a pre-phase of low carb diets before actually starting the diet itself, to allow your body to adjust and re-orient itself to the coming changes.

  This fasting method is comprised of two phases. Namely the Building phase (Time between first and last meal) and the cleaning phase (Time between last and first meal). Try to maintain a time period of 12 hour between the cleansing phase and 8 hours between the building phases for a start. Then keep on growing from that.

- Make sure to keep your sodium intake in check to avoid future problems during your Ketogenic journey. Easy steps may include
    - Drinking organic broth if possible
    - Taking a just a pinch of pink salt with you consumed meals
    - Adding about ¼ teaspoon of pink salt to 16 ounces of water consumed
    - Adding vegetables such as kelp to your dishes
    - Eating up vegetables such as cucumber or celery for a more natural approach to sodium replenishment
- Try to maintain a proper exercise regime while going on your Ketogenic Diet, as it will not only help to make your Keto diet much more effective but also put a positive impact on your overall health while allowing you to maintain a more stable and prolonged state of ketosis.

    A sample exercise routine may include

    - Monday: Resistance training for upper body (20 minutes)
    - Tuesday: Resistance training for Lower Body (20 minutes)
    - Wednesday: Long walk of 30 minutes
    - Thursday: Resistance training for upper body (20 minutes)
    - Friday: Resistance training for Lower Body (20 minutes)
    - Sat/Sun: Recreational time.

# Chapter 2: Air Fryer Basics

## What are advantages of Cosori Air Fryer

In the long run, The Cosori Air Fryer will significantly cut down your Oil Intake, in fact, researches have shown that it has the capacity to cut it down by almost 80%! This is possibly the healthiest advantage that you will experience while using an Air Fryer. However, if you want to go even further:

- Prepare awesome and extremely delicious meals without any hassle
- Unlike most other bulky cooking appliances, cleaning the Cosori is extremely easy (as seen the next segment)
- Since the Air Fryer helps to cut down oil, cooking with the Fryer will significantly contribute in weight loss and allow you to stay healthy
- If you are in a rush, the Air Fryer will greatly be advantageous to you as well since it allows you to cook extremely fast!

## Learning to Keep Your Device Clean

Just like any other cooking appliance, the Cosori also has the potential accumulate dirt and debris as you keep using it for prolonged period of time. If you don't take care of it properly, the appliance's life might get reduced. Therefore, it is highly advised that you keep your appliance as much clean as possible to get the best experience out of it.

The following simple steps should help you keep your Fryer clean with ease.

- It is very normal for meals to leave a sticky residue inside the cooking basket of the fryer. An easy way to deal with this is to use specialized detergents or soap that are designed to dissolve oil.
- For maximum effect, try to soak the detergent mixed water for a few minutes before thoroughly rinsing it under hot water.
- Always keep in mind that metal utensils and cleaning brushes may leave scratches on the body of the Fryer. So, refrain yourself from using those.
- Make sure to complete cool down your Air Fryer and wait for 30 minutes prior to washing it

And on the topic of cleaning, you should remember the following steps while cleaning up your appliance:

- Remove the power cable from the wall and make sure that the device is completely cooled.
- Wipe out the external part of the Fryer using a moist cloth dipped in mild detergent.
- Clean the outer basket and the fryer basket and using hot water (mixed with mild detergent) and a soft sponge.
- Clean the inner part of the appliance using hot water (with mild detergent) and a soft sponge.
- If you find that some residue is stuck in the heating element, then you may use a cleaning brush to clear them out.

## Understanding the Science behind Air Fryer

Since you will be spending a lot of time with this appliance, perhaps it would be wise if you knew how the Air Fryer process actually works right?

Well, it's pretty simple if you think about it.

The keyword here is "Air"

Most other conventional cooking appliances tend to cook their meal by using some sort of heater that passes heat through the meal through a process known as conduction. This basically transfer heat to the meal on touch.

An Air Fryer on the other hand, does its cooking through a process called "Convection" where air is heated up and circulated throughout the food.

During your journey into the various super markets looking for an Air Fryer, you have most definitely seen the word "Rapid Air Technology" countless times. That actually refers to a very delicately designed process which the Air Fryer uses to cook its food.

The Air Is sucked up the intake chamber and the appliance gets heated up.

## Bowl

Prep Time: 5 minutes

Cooking Time: 10 minutes

Ingredients:

- 8 chestnut mushrooms
- 8 tomatoes, halved
- 1 garlic clove, crushed
- 4 rashers smoked back bacon
- 7 ounces baby leaf spinach
- 4 whole eggs
- Chipotle as needed

Directions:

1. Pre-heat your Air Fryer to 392 degrees F
2. Take the Air Fryer cooking basket and add mushrooms, tomatoes and garlic
3. Spray with oil and season well
4. Add bacon, chipotle to the Air Fryer and cook for 10 minutes
5. Take a microwave proof bowl and add spinach, heat until wilt
6. Add wilt spinach into the microwave proof bowl
7. Crack the eggs the bowl and Air Fry for 2-3 minutes at 320 degrees F

8. Serve cooked eggs with bacon, enjoy!

**Nutritional Contents:**

- Calories: 341
- Fat: 27g
- Carbohydrates: 10g
- Protein: 13g

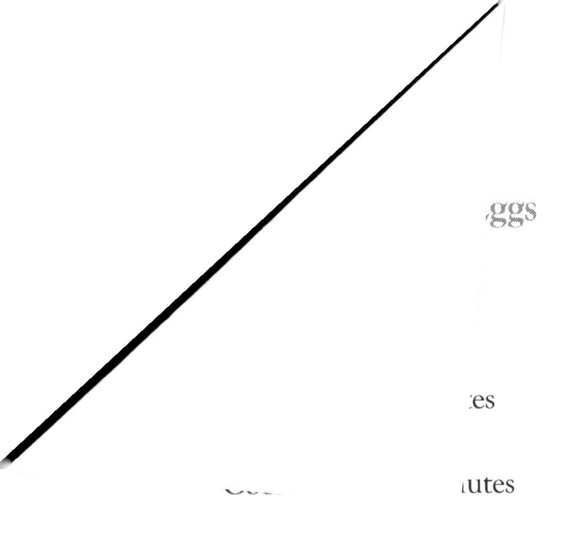

Ingredients:

- 2 whole eggs
- 2 tablespoons milk
- 1 teaspoons parmesan cheese
- 1 tomato, chopped
- Salt and pepper to taste
- 1 bacon slice
- Parsley, chopped

Directions:

1. Pre-heat your Fryer to 350-degree Fahrenheit for about 3 minutes.
2. Cut up the bacon into small portions and divide them amongst ramekins.
3. Dice up tomatoes and divide them amongst ramekins as well.
4. Crack an egg into the dishes and add 1 tablespoon of milk into the dishes.
5. Season the ramekins with pepper and salt.
6. Sprinkle ½ a teaspoon of parmesan and transfer the ramekins to your cooking basket.
7. Cook for 7 minutes and serve with a garnish of parsley.
8. Enjoy!

Nutritional Contents:

- Calories: 473
- Fat: 23g
- Carbohydrates: 6g
- Protein: 5g

## Morning Paneer Pizza

Serving: 4

Prep Time: 15 minutes

Cook Time: 10 minutes

### Ingredients:

- 7 and ¼ ounces Paneer
- ¼ onion
- 1 cube cheese
- ½ carrot
- Salt and pepper to taste
- ¼ tomato
- 1 capsicum
- 1 teaspoon corn

### Directions:

1. Pre-heat your fryer to 360-degree F.
2. Wash and dry your paneer.
3. Mix flour with water and make and knead to make nice dough.
4. Add paneer to the dough and knead again.
5. Take a bowl and make a filling of onion, tomato and carrot.
6. Add capsicum, salt and pepper to the mixture.
7. Transfer the mixture to your kneaded dough and spread carefully.
8. Transfer the prepared pizza to your Air Fryer and bake for 3 minutes.

9. Serve and enjoy with a garnish of your favorite herbs.
10. Enjoy!

Nutritional Contents:

- Calories: 334
- Fat: 30g
- Carbohydrates: 1g
- Protein: 18g

## Cheesed Up Omelette

Serving: 1

Prep Time: 5 minutes

Cook Time: 10 minutes

### Ingredients:

- 2 eggs
- Pepper
- Grated Cheddar
- Onion

1. Coconut Amino

### Directions:

2. Preheat your Air Fryer up to 340-degree F
3. Clean and chop onion
4. Take a plate and cover with 2 teaspoons amino
5. Transfer into the Air Fryer and cook for 8 minutes
6. Beat eggs and add pepper with salt
7. Pour the egg mixture on onions and cook the mix in your Air Fryer for 3 minutes more
8. Add cheddar cheese and bake for 2 minutes more
9. Serve with fresh basil leaves

### Nutritional Contents:

- Calories: 396

- Fat: 32g
- Carbohydrates: 1g
- Protein: 27g

## Simple Cooked Egg

Serving: 6

Prep Time: 1 minute

Cook Time: 15 minutes

### Ingredients:

- 6 large eggs

### Directions:

1. Preheat your air fryer 300-degree F.
2. Put the eggs in a single layer in your air fryer basket carefully.
3. Bake for at least 8 minutes for a slightly runny yolk.
4. Or 12 to 15 minutes for a firmer yolk.
5. Using tongs remove the eggs from the air fryer carefully.
6. Then take a bowl of very cold water and immediately place them in it.
7. Let the eggs stand in the cold water for 5 minutes, then gently crack the shell under water.
8. After that, let the eggs stand for another minute or two, then peel and eat.
9. Enjoy!

### Nutritional Contents:

- Calories: 63
- Fat: 4g
- Carbohydrates: <1g
- Protein: 6g

## Ham and Quiche in A Cup

Serving: 18

Prep Time: 10 minutes

Cook Time: 15 minutes

### Ingredients:

- 5 whole eggs
- 2 and ¼ ounces ham
- 1 cup milk
- 1/8 teaspoon pepper
- 1 and ½ cup Swiss cheese
- ¼ teaspoon salt
- ¼ cup Green onion
- ½ teaspoon thyme

### Directions:

1. Pre-heat your Fryer to 350-degree F.
2. Crack your eggs in a bowl and beat it well.
3. Add thyme onion, salt, Swiss cheese pepper, milk to the beaten eggs.
4. Prepare your baking forms for muffins and place ham slices in each baking form.
5. Cover the ham with egg mixture.
6. Transfer to Air Fryer and bake for 15 minutes.
7. Serve and enjoy!

### Nutritional Contents:

- Calories: 80
- Fat: 5g
- Carbohydrates: 0g
- Protein: 7g

## Japanese Omelette

Serving: 1

Prep Time: 10 minutes

Cook Time: 10 minutes

### Ingredients:

- 1 small Japanese tofu
- 3 eggs
- Pepper
- 1 teaspoon coriander
- 1 teaspoon cumin
- 2 tablespoons coconut amino
- 2 tablespoons green onion
- Olive oil

### Directions:

1. Preheat your Air Fryer up to 400-degree F
2. Clean and chop onion
3. Beat eggs and add with amino, pepper, oil, salt and mix
4. Take special baking forms and cut tofu into cubes and place in the baking forms
5. Add egg mixture
6. Transfer into the Air Fryer and cook for 10 minutes
7. Serve with fresh herbs
8. Enjoy!

Nutritional Contents:

- Calories: 300
- Fat: 40g
- Carbohydrates: 14g
- Protein: 72g

# Chapter 4: Poultry Recipes

## Chicken and Sage Scallops

Serving: 4

Prep Time: 5 minutes

Cooking Time: 10 minutes

### Ingredients:

- 4 skinless chicken breasts
- 2 and ½ ounces almond meal
- 1-ounce parmesan, grated
- 6 sage leaves, chopped
- 1 and ¾ ounces almond flour
- 2 eggs, beaten

### Directions:

1. Take cling paper and wrap chicken with cling wrap
2. Beat into ½ cm thickness using a rolling pin
3. Take separate bowls add parmesan, sage, almond meal, flour and beaten eggs into the different bowls
4. Take chicken and dredge into flour, eggs, bread crumbs and finally parmesan
5. Pre-heat your Fryer to 392 degrees F
6. Take the basket out and spray chicken with oil on both sides
7. Cook chicken for 5 minutes each side until golden

8. Serve and enjoy!

**Nutritional Contents:**

- Calories: 264
- Fat: 18g
- Carbohydrates: 3g
- Protein: 19g

## Cool Cheese Dredged Chicken

Serving: 4

Prep Time: 10 minutes

Cooking Time: 10 minutes

### Ingredients:

- 2-piece (6 ounces each) chicken breast, fat trimmed and sliced up in half
- 6 tablespoons seasoned breadcrumbs
- 2 tablespoons parmesan, grated
- 1 tablespoon melted butter
- 2 tablespoons low-fat mozzarella cheese
- ½ cup marinara sauce
- Cooking spray as needed

### Directions:

1. Pre-heat your Air Fryer to 390-degree Fahrenheit for about 9 minutes
2. Take the cooking basket and spray it evenly with cooking spray
3. Take a small bowl and add breadcrumbs and parmesan cheese
4. Mix them well
5. Take another bowl and add the butter, melt it in your microwave
6. Brush the chicken pieces with the butter and dredge them into the breadcrumb mix
7. Once the fryer is ready, place 2 pieces of your prepared chicken breast and spray the top a bit of oil

8. Cook for about 6 minutes
9. Turn them over and top them up with 1 tablespoon of Marinara and 1 and a ½ tablespoon of shredded mozzarella
10. Cook for 3 minutes more until the cheese has completely melted
11. Keep the cooked breasts on the side and repeat with the remaining pieces

Nutritional Contents:

- Calories: 244
- Fat: 14g
- Carbohydrates: 15g
- Protein: 12g

## Spiced Up Air Fried Buffalo Wings

Serving: 4

Prep Time: 10 minutes

Cooking Time: 30 minutes

### Ingredients:

- 4 pounds chicken wings
- ½ cup cayenne pepper sauce
- ½ cup coconut oil
- 1 tablespoon Worcestershire sauce
- 1 teaspoon salt

### Directions:

1. Take a mixing cup and add cayenne pepper sauce, coconut oil, Worcestershire sauce and salt
2. Mix well and keep it on the side
3. Pat the chicken dry and transfer to your fryer
4. Cook for 25 minutes at 380-degree F, making sure to shake the basket once
5. Increase the temperature to 400-degree F and cook for 5 minutes more
6. Remove them and dump into a large sized mixing bowl
7. Add the prepared sauce and toss well
8. Serve with celery sticks and enjoy!

### Nutritional Contents:

- Calories: 244

- Fat: 20g
- Carbohydrates: 6g
- Protein: 8g

## Creamy Onion Chicken

Serving: 4

Prep Time: 30 minutes

Cook Time: 30 minutes

### Ingredients:

- 4 chicken breasts
- 1 and ½ cup onion soup mix
- 1 cup mushroom soup

1. ½ cup cream

### Directions:

2. Pre-heat your Fryer to 400-degree F.
3. Take a frying pan and place it over low heat.
4. Add mushrooms, onion mix and cream.
5. Heat up the mixture for 1 minute.
6. Pour the warm mixture over chicken and let it sit for 25 minutes.
7. Transfer your marinade chicken to Air Fryer cooking basket and cook for 30 minutes.
8. Serve with remaining cream and enjoy!

### Nutritional Contents:

- Calories: 282
- Fat: 4g
- Carbohydrates: 55g
- Protein: 8g

## Baked Coconut Chicken

Serving: 6

Prep Time: 5 minutes

Cook Time: 12 minutes

Ingredients:

- 2 large eggs
- 2 teaspoons garlic powder
- 1 teaspoon salt
- 1/2 teaspoon ground black pepper
- ¾ cup coconut amino
- ¾ cup shredded coconut
- 1-pound chicken tenders
- Cooking spray

Directions:

1. Pre-heat your fryer to 400-degree Fahrenheit.
2. Take a large sized baking sheet and spray it with cooking spray.
3. Take a wide dish and add garlic powder, eggs, pepper and salt.
4. Whisk well until everything is combined.
5. Add the almond meal and coconut and mix well.
6. Take your chicken tenders and dip them in egg followed by dipping in the coconut mix.
7. Shake off any excess.

8. Transfer them to your fryer and spray the tenders with a bit of oil.
9. Cook for 12-14 minutes until you have a nice golden-brown texture.
10. Enjoy!

Nutritional Contents:

- Calories: 175
- Fat: 1g
- Carbohydrates: 3g
- Protein: 0g

## Lemon Pepper Chicken

Serving: 2

Prep Time: 3 minutes

Cook Time: 15 minutes

### Ingredients:

- 1 chicken breast
- 2 lemon, juiced and rind reserved
- 1 tablespoon chicken seasoning
- 1 teaspoon garlic puree
- Handful of peppercorns
- Salt and pepper to taste

### Directions:

1. Pre-heat your fryer to 352-degree F.
2. Take a large sized sheet of silver foil and work on top, add all of the seasoning alongside the lemon rind.
3. Lay out the chicken breast onto a chopping board and trim any fat and little bones.
4. Season each side with the pepper and salt.
5. Rub the chicken seasoning on both sides well.
6. Place on your silver foil sheet and rub.
7. Seal it up tightly.
8. Slap it with rolling pin and flatten it.
9. Place it in your fryer and cook for 15 minutes until the center is fully cooked.

10. Serve and enjoy!

**Nutritional Contents:**

- Calories: 301
- Fat: 22g
- Carbohydrates: 11g
- Protein: 23g

## Crunchy Mustard Chicken

Serving: 4

Prep Time: 20 minutes

Cook Time: 50 minutes

### Ingredients:

- 4 garlic cloves
- 8 chicken slices
- 1 tablespoon thyme leaves
- ½ cup dry wine vinegar
- Salt as needed
- ½ cup Dijon mustard
- 2 cups almond meal
- 2 tablespoons melted butter
- 1 tablespoon lemon zest
- 2 tablespoons olive oil

### Directions:

1. Pre-heat your Air Fryer to 350-degree F
2. Take a bowl and add garlic, salt, cloves, almond meal, pepper, olive oil, melted butter and lemon zest
3. Take another bowl and mix mustard and wine
4. Place chicken slices in the wine mixture and then in the crumb mixture

5. Transfer prepared chicken to your Air Fryer cooking basket and cook for 40 minutes.
6. Serve and enjoy!

**Nutritional Contents:**

- Calories: 762
- Fat: 24g
- Carbohydrates: 3g
- Protein: 76g

## Caprese Chicken with Balsamic Sauce

Serving: 6

Prep Time: 5 minutes

Cook Time: 25 minutes

### Ingredients:

- 6 chicken breasts
- 6 basil leaves
- ¼ cup balsamic vinegar
- 6 slices tomato
- 1 tablespoon butter
- 6 slices mozzarella cheese

### Directions:

1. Pre-heat your Fryer to 400-degree F.
2. Take a frying and place it over medium heat, add butter and balsamic vinegar and let it melt.
3. Cover the chicken meat with the marinade.
4. Transfer chicken to your Air Fryer cooking basket and cook for 20 minutes.
5. Cover cooked chicken with basil, tomato slices and cheese.

### Nutritional Contents:

- Calories: 740
- Fat: 54g
- Carbohydrates: 4g
- Protein: 30g

## Grilled Hawaiian Chicken

Serving: 2

Prep Time: 10 minutes

Cook Time: 15 minutes

### Ingredients:

- 4 chicken breasts
- 2 garlic cloves
- ½ cup ketchup, Keto-friendly
- ½ teaspoon ginger
- ½ cup coconut amino
- 2 tablespoons red wine vinegar
- ½ cup pineapple juice
- 2 tablespoons apple cider vinegar

### Directions:

1. Pre-heat your Air Fryer to 360-degree F.
2. Take a bowl and mix in ketchup, pineapple juice, cider vinegar, ginger.
3. Take a frying and place it over low heat, add sauce and let it heat up.
4. Cover chicken with the amino and vinegar, pour hot sauce on top.
5. Let the chicken sit for 15 minutes to marinade.
6. Transfer chicken to your Air Fryer and bake for 15 minutes.
7. Serve and enjoy!

### Nutritional Contents:

- Calories: 200
- Fat: 3g
- Carbohydrates: 10g
- Protein: 29g

# Chapter 5: Appetizers and Sliders Recipes

## Bacon and Asparagus Spears

Serving: 4

Prep Time: 15 minutes

Cooking Time: 8 minutes

### Ingredients:

- 20 spears asparagus
- 4 bacon slices
- 1 tablespoon olive oil
- 1 tablespoon sesame oil
- 1 garlic clove, crushed

### Directions:

1. Pre-heat your Air Fryer to 380 degrees F
2. Take a small bowl and add oil, crushed garlic and mix
3. Separate asparagus into 4 bunches and wrap them in bacon
4. Brush wraps with oil and garlic mix, transfer to your Air Fryer basket
5. Cook for 8 minutes

### Nutritional Contents:

- Calories: 175
- Fat: 15g
- Carbohydrates: 6g
- Protein: 5g

## Healthy Low Carb Fish Nugget

Serving: 4

Prep Time: 5 minutes

Cooking Time: 10 minutes

### Ingredients:

- 1-pound fresh cod
- 2 tablespoons olive oil
- ½ cup almond flour
- 2 larges finely beaten eggs
- 1-2 cups almond meal
- Salt as needed

### Directions:

1. Pre-heat your Air Fryer to 388 degrees F
2. Take a food processor and add olive oil, almond meal, salt and blend
3. Take three bowls and add almond flour, almond meal, beaten eggs individually
4. Take cods and cut them into slices of 1-inch thickness and 2-inch length
5. Dredge slices into flour, eggs and in crumbs
6. Transfer nuggets to Air Fryer cooking basket and cook for 10 minutes until golden

### Nutritional Contents:

- Calories: 196
- Fat: 14g
- Carbohydrates: 6g
- Protein: 14g

## Baked Mediterranean Veggies

Serving: 8

Prep Time: 20 minutes

Cook Time: 45 minutes

### Ingredients:

- Olive oil as needed
- 18 ounces eggplant
- 4 garlic cloves
- 18 ounces zucchini
- Thyme sprig
- 18 ounces bell pepper
- Salt and pepper to taste
- 4 whole onions
- Bay leaf
- 18 ounces tomatoes
- Almond flour

### Directions:

1. Pre-heat your fryer to 380-degree F
2. Cut tomatoes and bake them for 2 minutes
3. Mix eggplant with olive oil and spices, transfer to Air Fryer and cook for 4 minutes
4. Cook zucchini in your Air Fryer for 4 minutes (with olive oil)

5. Add tomatoes, bell pepper to the mix and bake for 2 minutes more (add more olive oil and almond flour if you prefer)
6. Serve and enjoy!

Nutrition Contents:

- Calories: 279
- Fat: 13g
- Carbohydrates: 10g
- Protein: 10g

## Fried Up Pumpkin Seeds

Serving: 2

Prep Time: 10 minutes

Cooking Time: 60 minutes

### Ingredients:

- 1 and ½ cups pumpkin seeds
- Olive oil as needed
- 1 and ½ teaspoons salt
- 1 teaspoon smoked paprika

### Directions:

1. Cut pumpkin and scrape out seeds and flesh
2. Separate flesh from seeds and rinse the seeds under cold water
3. Bring 2 quarter of salted water to boil and add seeds, boil for 10 minutes
4. Drain seeds and spread them on a kitchen towel
5. Dry for 20 minutes
6. Pre-heat your fryer to 350 degrees F
7. Take a bowl and add seeds, smoked paprika and olive oil
8. Season with salt and transfer to your Air Fryer cooking basket
9. Cook for 35 minutes, enjoy!

### Nutritional Contents:

- Calories: 237
- Fat: 21g
- Carbohydrates: 4g
- Protein: 12g

## Mixed Masala Cashew Dish

Serving: 2

Prep Time: 5 minutes

Cook Time: 10 minutes

### Ingredients:

- 8 ounces Greek yogurt
- 2 teaspoons mango powder
- 8 and ¾ ounces cashew nuts
- Salt and pepper to taste
- 1 teaspoon coriander powder
- ½ teaspoon masala powder
- ½ teaspoon black pepper powder

### Directions:

1. Pre-heat your Fryer to 240 degrees F
2. Make a mix of the powders and season with salt and pepper
3. Add cashews to the mix and toss
4. Transfer the cashews and marinade to your Air Fryer and cook for 15 minutes.
5. Serve with a garnish of basil

### Nutritional Contents:

- Calories: 140
- Fat: 8g
- Carbohydrates: 11g
- Protein: 4g

## Decisive Tiger Shrimp Platter

Serving: 6

Prep Time: 5 minutes

Cook Time: 10 minutes

### Ingredients:

- 1 ¼ pound tiger shrimp, or a count of about 16 to 20
- ¼ teaspoons cayenne pepper
- ½ teaspoons old bay seasoning
- ¼ teaspoons smoked paprika
- pinch of salt
- 1 tablespoon olive oil

### Directions:

1. Pre-heat your Fryer to 390-degree Fahrenheit
2. Take a bowl and add the listed ingredients
3. Mix well
4. Transfer the shrimp to your fryer cooking basket and cook for 5 minutes
5. Remove and serve the shrimp over cauliflower rice if preferred

### Nutrition Values (Per Serving)

- Calories:251
- Carbohydrate: 3g
- Protein: 17g
- Fat: 19g

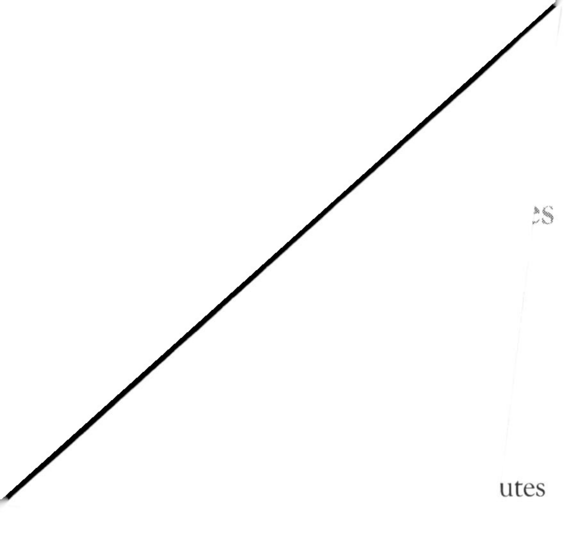

utes

Ingredients:

- 1 medium red bell pepper, cut into small portions
- 1 medium yellow pepper, cut into small portions
- 1 medium green bell pepper, cut into small portions
- 3 tablespoons balsamic vinegar
- 2 tablespoons olive oil
- 1 tablespoon garlic, minced
- ½ teaspoon dried basil
- ½ teaspoon dried parsley
- Salt and pepper to taste

Directions:

1. Take a mixing bowl and add diced peppers
2. Mix them and add olive oil, garlic, balsamic vinegar, basil, parsley and mix well
3. Season with salt and pepper
4. Cover and let it chill for 30 minutes
5. Pre-heat your Fryer to 390-degree F
6. Transfer the peppers to your Air Fryer and cook for 10-15 minutes
7. Serve and enjoy!

Nutrition Contents:

- Calories: 148
- Fat: 7g
- Carbohydrates: 10g
- Protein: 5g

# Chapter 6: Vegetarian Recipes

## Squash and Cumin Chili

Serving: 4

Prep Time: 10 minutes

Cooking Time: 16 minutes

### Ingredients:

- 1 medium butternut squash
- 2 teaspoons cumin seeds
- 1 large pinch chili flakes
- 1 tablespoon olive oil
- 1 and ½ ounces pine nuts
- 1 small bunch fresh coriander, chopped

### Directions:

1. Take the squash and slice it
2. Remove seeds and cut into smaller chunks
3. Take a bowl and add chunked squash, spice and oil
4. Mix well
5. Pre-heat your Fryer to 360 degrees F and add the squash to the cooking basket
6. Roast for 20 minutes, making sure to shake the basket from time to time to avoid burning

7. Take pan and place it over medium heat, add pine nuts to the pan and dry toast for 2 minutes
8. Sprinkle nuts on top of squash and serve
9. Enjoy!

Nutritional Contents:

- Calories: 414
- Fat: 15g
- Carbohydrates: 10g
- Protein: 16g

## Fried Up Avocados

Serving: 6

Prep Time: 10 minutes

Cooking Time: 20 minutes

### Ingredients:

- ½ cup almond meal
- ½ teaspoon salt
- 1 Hass avocado, peeled, pitted and sliced
- Aquafaba from one bean can (bean liquid)

### Directions:

1. Take a shallow bowl and add almond meal, salt
2. Pour aquafaba in another bowl, dredge avocado slices in aquafaba and then into the crumbs to get a nice coating
3. Arrange them in a single layer in your Air Fryer cooking basket, don't overlap
4. Cook for 10 minutes at 390 degrees F, give the basket a shake and cook for 5 minutes more
5. Serve and enjoy!

### Nutritional Contents:

- Calories: 356
- Fat: 14g
- Carbohydrates: 8g
- Protein: 23g

## Hearty Green Beans

Serving: 6

Prep Time: 5 minutes

Cooking Time: 10-15 minutes

### Ingredients:

- 1-pound green beans, washed and de-stemmed
- 1 lemon
- Pinch of salt
- ¼ teaspoon oil

### Directions:

1. Add beans to your Air Fryer cooking basket
2. Squeeze a few drops of lemon
3. Season with salt and pepper
4. Drizzle olive oil on top
5. Cook for 10-12 minutes at 400 degrees F
6. Once done, serve and enjoy!

### Nutritional Contents:

- Calories: 84
- Fat: 5g
- Carbohydrates: 7g
- Protein: 2g

## Parmesan Cabbage Wedges

Serving: 4

Prep Time: 5 minutes

Cook Time: 20 minutes

### Ingredients:

- ½ a head cabbage
- 2 cups parmesan
- 4 tablespoons melted butter
- Salt and pepper to taste

### Directions:

1. Pre-heat your Air Fryer to 380-degree F.
2. Take a bowl and add melted butter and season with salt and pepper.
3. Cover cabbages with your melted butter.
4. Coat cabbages with parmesan.
5. Transfer the coated cabbages to your Air Fryer and bake for 20 minutes.
6. Serve with cheesy sauce and enjoy!

### Nutrition Contents:

- Calories: 108
- Fat: 7g
- Carbohydrates: 11g
- Protein: 2g

## Extreme Zucchini Fries

Serving: 4

Prep Time: 10 minutes

Cook Time: 15-20 minutes

### Ingredients:

- 3 medium zucchinis, sliced
- 2 egg whites
- ½ cup seasoned almond meal
- 2 tablespoons grated parmesan cheese
- Cooking spray as needed
- ¼ teaspoon garlic powder
- Salt and pepper to taste

### Directions:

1. Pre-heat your Fryer to 425-degree F.
2. Take the Air Fryer cooking basket and place a cooling rack.
3. Coat the rack with cooking spray.
4. Take a bowl and add egg whites, beat it well and season with some pepper and salt.
5. Take another bowl and add garlic powder, cheese and almond meal
6. Take the Zucchini sticks and dredge them in the egg and finally breadcrumbs.
7. Transfer the Zucchini to your cooking basket and spray a bit of oil.
8. Bake for 20 minutes and serve with Ranch sauce.
9. Enjoy!

**ition Contents:**

- Calories: 367
- Fat: 28g
- Carbohydrates: 5g
- Protein: 4g

## Easy Fried Tomatoes

Serving: 3

Prep Time: 5 minutes

Cook Time: 10 minutes

### Ingredients:

- 1 green tomato
- ¼ tablespoon Creole seasoning
- Salt and pepper to taste
- ¼ cup almond flour
- ½ cup buttermilk
- Bread crumbs as needed

### Directions:

1. Add flour to your plate and take another plate and add buttermilk
2. Cut tomatoes and season with salt and pepper
3. Make a mix of creole seasoning and crumbs
4. Take tomato slice and cover with flour, place in buttermilk and then into crumbs
5. Repeat with all tomatoes
6. Pre-heat your fryer to 400-degree F
7. Cook the tomato slices for 5 minutes
8. Serve with basil and enjoy!

### Nutrition Contents:

- Calories: 166

- Fat: 12g
- Carbohydrates: 11g
- Protein: 3g

## Roasted Up Brussels

Serving: 4

Prep Time: 10 minutes

Cook Time: 15 minutes

### Ingredients:

- 1 block Brussels sprouts
- ½ teaspoon garlic
- 2 teaspoons olive oil
- ½ teaspoon pepper
- Salt as needed

### Directions:

1. Pre-heat your Fryer to 390-degree F.
2. Remove leaves off the chokes, leaving only the head.
3. Wash and dry the sprouts well.
4. Make a mixture of olive oil, salt and pepper with garlic.
5. Cover sprouts with marinade and let them rest for 5 minutes.
6. Transfer coated sprouts to Air Fryer and cook for 15 minutes.
7. Serve and enjoy!

### Nutritional Contents:

- Calories: 43
- Fat: 2g
- Carbohydrates: 5g
- Protein: 2g

## Roasted Brussels and Pine Nuts

Serving: 6

Prep Time: 10 minutes

Cook Time: 35 minutes

### Ingredients:

- 15 ounces Brussels sprouts
- 1 tablespoon olive oil
- 1 and ¾ ounces raisins, drained
- Juice of 1 orange
- 1 and ¾ ounces toasted pine nuts

### Directions:

1. Take a pot of boiling water and add sprouts and boil them for 4 minutes.
2. Transfer the sprouts to cold water and drain them well.
3. Place them in a freezer and cool them.
4. Take your raisins and soak them in orange juice for 20 minutes.
5. Pre-heat your Air Fryer to a temperature of 392-degree F.
6. Take a pan and pour oil and stir the sprouts.
7. Take the sprouts and transfer them to your Air Fryer.
8. Roast for 15 minutes.
9. Serve the sprouts with pine nuts, orange juice and raisins!

### Nutrition Contents:

- Calories: 260
- Fat: 20g
- Carbohydrates: 10g
- Protein: 7g

## Low Calorie Beets Dish

Serving: 2

Prep Time: 10 minutes

Cook Time: 10 minutes

### Ingredients:

- 4 whole beets
- 1 tablespoon balsamic vinegar
- 1 tablespoon olive oil
- Salt and pepper to taste
- 2 springs rosemary

### Directions:

1. Wash your beets and peel them
2. Cut beets into cubes
3. Take a bowl and mix in rosemary, pepper, salt, vinegar
4. Cover beets with the prepared sauce
5. Coat the beets with olive oil
6. Pre-heat your Fryer to 400-degree F
7. Transfer beets to Air Fryer cooking basket and cook for 10 minutes
8. Serve with your cheese sauce and enjoy!

### Nutrition Contents:

- Calories: 149
- Fat: 1g
- Carbohydrates: 5g
- Protein: 30g

## Broccoli and Parmesan Dish

Serving: 4

Prep Time: 5 minutes

Cook Time: 20 minutes

Ingredients:

- 1 head fresh broccoli
- 1 tablespoon olive oil
- 1 lemon, juiced
- Salt and pepper to taste
- 1-ounce parmesan cheese, grated

Directions:

1. Wash broccoli thoroughly and cut them into florets.
2. Add the listed ingredients to your broccoli and mix well.
3. Pre-heat your fryer to 365-degree F.
4. Air fry broccoli for 20 minutes.
5. Serve and enjoy!

Nutrition Contents:

- Calories: 114
- Fat: 6g
- Carbohydrates: 10 g
- Protein: 7g

# ish and Seafood Recipes

## le Grilled Fish and Cheese

Serving: 4

Prep Time: 5 minutes

Cooking Time: 7 minutes

**Ingredients:**

- 1 bunch basil
- 2 garlic cloves
- 1 tablespoon olive oil (for cooking)
- ¼ cup olive oil (extra)
- 1 tablespoon parmesan cheese
- Salt and pepper to taste
- 2 tablespoons Pinenuts
- 6 ounces white fish fillet

**Directions:**

1. Brush the fish fillets with oil and season with some pepper and salt
2. Pre-heat your Air Fryer to a temperature of 356-degree Fahrenheit
3. Carefully transfer the fillets to your Air Fryer cooking basket
4. Cook for about 8 minutes
5. Take a small bowl and add basil, olive oil, pine nuts, garlic, parmesan cheese and blend using your hand

6. Serve this mixture with the fish!

Nutritional Contents:

- Calories: 344
- Fat: 26g
- Carbohydrates: 7g
- Protein: 21g

## Lovely Garlic Flavored Prawn

Serving: 2

Prep Time: 5 minutes

Cooking Time: 10 minutes

### Ingredients:

- 15 fresh prawns
- 1 tablespoon olive oil
- 1 teaspoon chili powder
- 1 tablespoon black pepper
- 1 tablespoon chili sauce, Keto-Friendly
- 1 garlic clove, minced
- Salt as needed

### Directions:

1. Pre-heat your Air Fryer to 356 degrees F
2. Wash prawns thoroughly and rinse them
3. Take a mixing bowl and add washed prawn, chili powder, oil, garlic, pepper, chili sauce and stir the mix
4. Transfer prawn to Air Fryer and cook for 8 minutes

### Nutritional Contents:

- Calories: 131
- Fat: 10g
- Carbohydrates: 4g
- Protein: 7g

## Fennel and Cod

Serving: 4

Prep Time: 5 minutes

Cook Time: 10 minutes

### Ingredients:

- 2 cod fillets
- Salt and pepper to taste
- 1 cup grapes, halved
- ½ cup pecans
- 1 small fennel, sliced
- 3 cups kale, shredded
- 2 teaspoons balsamic vinegar
- 2 tablespoons extra virgin olive oil

### Directions:

1. Pre-heat your Fryer to 400-degree Fahrenheit and season your fillets with pepper and salt
2. Drizzle olive oil on top
3. Transfer the fillets to your cooking basket making sure that the ksin side is facing down
4. Fry for 10 minutes and remove them once done
5. Make an aluminum tent and allow them to cool
6. Take a bowl and add grapes, pecans, fennels

7. Drizzle olive oil and season with salt and pepper
8. Add the mix to your cooking basket and cook for 5 minutes
9. Dress them with balsamic vinegar and add olive oil
10. Season with some additional pepper and salt it you need, enjoy!

### Nutrition Values (Per Serving)

- Calories: 269
- Carbohydrate: 5g
- Protein: 32g
- Fat: 1g

## Fresh Broiled Tilapia

Serving: 4

Prep Time: 5 minutes

Cook Time: 10 minutes

### Ingredients:

- 1-pound tilapia fillets
- Old bay seasoning as needed
- Canola oil as needed
- Lemon pepper as needed
- Salt to taste
- Butter buds

### Directions:

1. Pre-heat your Fryer to 400-degree F.
2. Cover tilapia with oil.
3. Take a bowl and mix in salt, lemon pepper, butter buds, seasoning.
4. Cover your fish with the sauce.
5. Bake fillets for 10 minutes.
6. Serve and enjoy!

### Nutritional Contents:

- Calories: 177
- Fat: 10g
- Carbohydrates: 1.2g
- Protein: 25g

## Authentic Alaskan Crab Legs

Serving: 3

Prep Time: 15 minutes

Cook Time: 10 minutes

### Ingredients:

- 3 pounds crab legs
- 2 cups Butter, melted
- 1 cup water
- ½ teaspoon salt

### Directions:

1. Pre-heat your Fryer to 380-degree F.
2. Cover legs with water and salt.
3. Place crab legs in Air Fryer.
4. Bake for 10 minutes.
5. Melt butter and pour butter over your baked Crab Legs.
6. Enjoy!

### Nutrition Contents:

- Calories: 130
- Fat: 2g
- Carbohydrates: 0g
- Protein: 26g

## Bacon and Shrimp Wrap

Serving: 1

Prep Time: 10 minutes

Cook Time: 10 minutes

### Ingredients:

- 1 and a quarter pound of deveined shrimps
- 16 slices of 1 pound thinly sliced bacon

### Directions:

1. Take your bacon slices and wrap them up around the shrimp
2. Make sure to start from the bottom and go all way to the top
3. Repeat until all the shrimps are used up
4. Transfer them to your fridge and chill for 20 minutes
5. Pre-heat your fryer to 390-degree Fahrenheit
6. Take the shrimp and transfer them to the cooking basket, cook for 5-7 minutes
7. Enjoy!

### Nutrition Values (Per Serving)

- Calories: 40
- Carbohydrate: 9g
- Protein: 30g
- Fat: 40g

## Herbed Healthy Salmon

Serving: 3

Prep Time: 5 minutes

Cook Time: 16 minutes

### Ingredients:

- 2 salmon fillets
- 2 teaspoons garlic, minced
- 1 teaspoons olive oil
- 1 cup white wine vinegar
- 3 tablespoons coconut oil
- Salt as needed
- Dried Italian herbs

### Directions:

1. Pre-heat your fryer to 350-degree Fahrenheit
2. Pat the salmon pieces dry using a kitchen towel and season with salt
3. Transfer them to your fryer and cook for 6 minutes
4. Take a saucepan and add olive oil, heat it up over medium heat
5. Add garlic to the pan and stir cook
6. Add white wine vinegar and bring the mix to a boil, cook for 5 minutes
7. Stir in coconut oil and sprinkle Italian herb seasoning
8. Serve the salmon with this sauce
9. Enjoy!

Nutrition Values (Per Serving)

- Calories: 504
- Carbohydrate: 8g
- Protein: 37g
- Fat: 36g

## Excellent Catfish

Serving: 4

Prep Time: 10 minutes

Cook Time: 20 minutes

### Ingredients:

- 4 catfish fillets
- ¼ cup of seasoned fish fry
- 1 tablespoon of olive oil
- 1 tablespoon of chopped parsley

### Directions:

1. Pre-heat your Fryer to 400-degree Fahrenheit
2. Take your catfish and rinse it well, pat it dry using kitchen towel
3. Take a large sized zip bag and add the fish and seasoning
4. Add a bit of olive oil and coat the fish, shake it well
5. Transfer the fillets to your Fryer and fry for 10 minutes
6. Flip it up and fry for 10 minutes more
7. Flip it for the last time and cook for 1-3 minutes
8. Top it up with parsley and enjoy!

### Nutrition Values (Per Serving)

- Calories: 199
- Carbohydrate: 14g
- Protein: 16g
- Fat: 12g

## Herbed Garlic Lobster Tails

Serving: 3

Prep Time: 15 minutes

Cook Time: 10 minutes

### Ingredients:

- 4-ounce lobster tails
- 1 teaspoon garlic, minced
- 1 tablespoon butter
- Salt and pepper to taste
- ½ tablespoon lemon juice

### Directions:

1. Take your food processor and add all the ingredients except lobster, blend well.
2. Wash your lobster and halve them using meat knife.
3. Clean the skin of lobsters.
4. Cover lobsters with marinade.
5. Pre-heat your Fryer t o380 degree F.
6. Transfer prepared lobster to Air Fryer and bake for 10 minutes.
7. Serve with some fresh herbs and enjoy!

### Nutrition Contents:

- Calories: 450
- Fat: 24g
- Carbohydrates: 12g
- Protein: 9g

# Chapter 8: Meat Recipes

## Chimichurri Sauce and Skirt Steak

Serving: 4

Prep Time: 30 minutes

Cooking Time: 10 minutes

**Ingredients:**

- 16 ounces skirt steak

Chimichurri Sauce

- 1 cup parsley, chopped
- ¼ cup mint, chopped
- 2 tablespoons oregano, chopped
- 3 garlic cloves, chopped
- 1 teaspoon crushed red pepper
- 1 tablespoon cumin, grounded
- 1 teaspoon cayenne pepper
- 2 teaspoons smoked paprika
- 1 teaspoon salt
- ¼ teaspoon pepper
- ¾ cup olive oil
- 3 tablespoons red wine vinegar

Directions:

1. Take a bowl and mix all of the Ingredients: listed under Chimichurri section a[illegible] mix them well
2. Cut the steak into 2 pieces of 8-ounce portions
3. Take a re-sealable bag and add ¼ cup of Chimichurri alongside the steak pieces and shake them to ensure that steak is coated well
4. Allow it to chill in your fridge for 2-24 hours
5. Remove the steak from the fridge 30 minutes prior to cooking
6. Pre-heat your Fryer to 390-degree Fahrenheit
7. Transfer the steak to your Fryer and cook for about 8-10 minutes if you are looking for a medium-rare finish
8. Garnish with 2 tablespoon of Chimichurri sauce and enjoy!

Nutritional Contents:

- Calories: 244
- Fat: 18g
- Carbohydrates: 7g
- Protein: 13g

## ...alls

...gredients:

- 1 small onion, chopped
- ¾ pounds ground beef
- 1 tablespoon fresh parsley, chopped
- ½ tablespoon fresh thyme leaves, chopped
- 1 whole egg
- 3 tablespoons almond meal
- Salt and pepper to taste

Directions:

1. Chop onion and keep them on the side
2. Take a bowl and add listed Ingredients: mix well (including onions)
3. Make 12 balls
4. Pre-heat your Air Fryer to 390 degrees F, transfer balls to the fryer
5. Cook for 8 minutes (in batches if needed) and transfer the balls to oven
6. Add tomatoes sauce and drown the balls
7. Transfer the dish to your Air Fryer and cook for 5 minutes at 300 degrees F
8. Stir and serve
9. Enjoy!

Nutritional Contents:

- Calories: 257
- Fat: 18g
- Carbohydrates: 6g
- Protein: 15g

ef

utes

Ingredien...

- 2 teaspoons olive oil
- 4-pound top round roast beef
- 1 teaspoon salt
- ¼ teaspoon fresh ground black pepper
- 1 teaspoon dried thyme
- ½ teaspoon rosemary, chopped
- 3 pounds red potatoes, halved
- Olive oil, fresh ground black pepper and salt to taste

Directions:

1. Pre-heat your Air Fryer to 360-degree F
2. Rub olive oil all over the beef
3. Take a bowl and add rosemary, thyme, salt and pepper
4. Mix well
5. Season the beef with the mixture and transfer the meat to your Fryer
6. Cook for 20 minutes
7. Add potatoes alongside some pepper and oil
8. Turn the roast alongside and add the potatoes to the basket

9. Cook for 20 minutes
10. Make sure to rotate the mixture from time to time
11. Cook until you have reached your desired temperature (130F for Rare, 140F for Medium and 160F for Well Done)
12. Once done, allow the meat to cool for 10 minutes
13. Pre-heat your Air Fryer to 400-degree Fahrenheit and keep cooking the potatoes for 10 minutes
14. Serve with the potatoes with the beef and enjoy!

Nutritional Contents:

- Calories: 523
- Fat: 63g
- Carbohydrates: 4g
- Protein: 37g

## Subtle Rib Eyes

Serving: 4

Prep Time: 5 minutes

Cook Time: 14 minutes

### Ingredients:

- 2 pounds rib eye steak
- 1 tablespoon olive oil
- Salt and pepper to taste

### Directions:

1. Pre-heat your fryer to 350-degree Fahrenheit.
2. Rub oil on both sides of the steak.
3. Season with salt and pepper.
4. Place the steaks in your Air Fryer and cook for 8 minutes.
5. Turn them over and cook for 8 minutes more.
6. Cook in batches.
7. Enjoy!

### Nutritional Contents:

- Calories: 305
- Fat: 24g
- Carbohydrates: 2g
- Protein: 21g

## Dreamy Beef Roast

Serving: 3

Prep Time: 10 minutes

Cook Time: 12 minutes

### Ingredients:

- 2 teaspoons olivc oil
- 4-pound top round roast beef
- 1 teaspoon salt
- ¼ teaspoon fresh ground black pepper
- 1 teaspoon dried thyme
- ½ teaspoon fresh rosemary, chopped
- 3 pounds red potatoes, halved
- Olive oil, fresh ground black pepper and salt for garnish

### Directions:

1. Pre-heat your Air Fryer to 360-degree F.
2. Rub olive oil all over the beef.
3. Take a bowl and add rosemary, thyme, salt and pepper.
4. Mix well.
5. Season the beef with the mixture and transfer the meat to your Fryer.
6. Cook for 20 minutes.
7. Add potatoes alongside some pepper and oil.
8. Turn the roast alongside and add the potatoes to the basket.

or 20 minutes.

Make sure to rotate the mixture from time to time.

11. Cook until you have reached your desired temperature (130F for Rare, 140F for Medium and 160F for Well done).
12. Once done, allow the meat to cool for 10 minutes.
13. Pre-heat your Air Fryer to 400-degree F and keep cooking the potatoes for 10 minutes.
14. Serve with the potatoes with the beef and enjoy!

**Nutritional Contents:**

- Calories: 183
- Fat: 5g
- Carbohydrates: 10g
- Protein: 11g

## Beefy Corned Beef

Serving: 3

Prep Time: 15 minutes

Cook Time: 40 minutes

### Ingredients:

- 2 stalks celery
- 1 tablespoon beef spice
- 4 carrots
- 12 ounces bottle beer
- 1 and ½ cups chicken broth
- 4 pounds corned beef

### Directions:

1. Pre-heat your Air Fryer to 380-degree F.
2. Cover beef with beer and let it sit for 20 minutes.
3. Chop carrots and onion.
4. Take a pot and place it over high heat, boil carrots, onion, beef in chicken broth.
5. Drain the boiled meat and transfer to Air Fryer cooking basket.
6. Place vegetables on top and cover with spices.
7. Bake for 30 minutes in your Air Fryer.
8. Serve and enjoy!

### Nutritional Contents:

- Calories: 320

- Fat: 22g
- Carbohydrates: 10g
- Protein: 21g

## Lovely Pork Chops

Serving: 4

Prep Time: 15 minutes

Cook Time: 25 minutes

### Ingredients:

- 8 pork chops
- ¼ teaspoon pepper
- 4 cups stuffing mix
- ½ teaspoon salt
- 2 tablespoons olive oil
- 4 garlic cloves
- 2 tablespoon sage leaves

### Directions:

1. Pre-heat your Air Fryer to 350-degree F.
2. Cut a hole in your pork chops.
3. Fill up your pork chops with stuffing mix.
4. Take a bowl and mix in sage leaves, garlic cloves, olive oil, salt and pepper.
5. Cover chops with marinade and let it sit for 10 minutes.
6. Transfer pork chops to Air Fryer cooking basket and bake for 25 minutes.
7. Serve and enjoy!

### Nutritional Contents:

- Calories: 118

- Fat: 7g
- Carbohydrates: 3g
- Protein: 13g

## Macadamia Roast

Serving: 4

Prep Time: 15 minutes

Cooking Time: 22 minutes

### Ingredients:

- 1 garlic clove
- 1 tablespoon olive oil
- 1 and ¼ pound rack of lamb
- Salt and pepper to taste

Macadamia Crusts

- 3 ounces unsalted macadamia crust
- 1 tablespoon almond meal
- 1 tablespoon fresh rosemary, chopped
- 1 whole egg

### Directions:

1. Chop up the garlic and toss it with some olive oil to create a garlic oil mix
2. Brush the lamb rack with this prepared oil
3. Season with pepper and salt
4. Pre-heat your Air Fryer to a temperature of 220-degree Fahrenheit
5. Chop up the macadamia nuts and them to a bowl
6. Add almond meal and rosemary and mix them well

7. Take another bowl and whisk eggs
8. Dredge the meat into the egg mix and drain excess egg
9. Coat the lamb rack with the macadamia crust and place them into the Air Fryer basket
10. Cook for about 30 minutes, making sure to increase the temperature of 390-degree Fahrenheit after 30 minutes
11. Cook for 5 minutes more
12. Remove the meat and allow it to cool
13. Cover with aluminum foil and allow it to sit for 10 minutes
14. Enjoy!

### Nutritional Contents:

- Calories: 301
- Fat: 31g
- Carbohydrates: 5g
- Protein: 33g

## Tasty Stroganoff of Beef

Serving: 3

Prep Time: 10 minutes

Cook Time: 10 minutes

### Ingredients:

- 1-pound thin steak
- 4 tablespoons butter
- Onion
- 1 cup sour cream
- 8 ounces mushrooms
- 4 cups beef broth

### Directions:

1. Add butter to a microwave container and microwave it to melt the butter.
2. Pre-heat your Fryer to 400-degree F.
3. Take a bowl and add melted butter, sliced mushrooms, cream, chopped onion and beef broth.
4. Transfer the steak to the mixture and let it marinade for 10 minutes.
5. Transfer steaks to Air Fryer cooking basket and bake for 10 minutes.
6. Serve and enjoy!

### Nutritional Contents:

- Calories: 361
- Fat: 16g

- Carbohydrates: 11g
- Protein: 35g

# Chapter 9: Dessert Recipes

## Jalapeno Poppers

Serving: 4

Prep Time: 5 minutes

Cooking Time: 10 minutes

### Ingredients:

- 10 jalapeno poppers, halved and deseeded
- 8 ounces cashew cream
- ¼ cup fresh parsley
- ¾ cup almond meal

### Directions:

1. Take a bowl and mix ½ of almond meal and cashew cream
2. Add parsley and stuff the pepper with the mixture
3. Press the top gently with remaining crumbs and make an even topping
4. Transfer to Air Fryer cooking basket and cook for 8 minutes at 370 degrees F
5. Let it cool and enjoy!

### Nutritional Contents:

- Calories: 456
- Fat: 60g
- Carbohydrates: 7g
- Protein: 15g

## Buffalo Cauliflower Bites

Serving: 6

Prep Time: 5 minutes

Cook Time: 5-8 minutes

### Ingredients

- 3 ounces of cauliflower finely sliced 12mm thick florets
- 1 tablespoon of olive oil
- Kosher Salt
- Freshly ground pepper

### Directions

1. Pre-heat your fryer to 390-degree Fahrenheit
2. Take a bowl and toss cauliflower, olive oil and season with a bit of salt and pepper
3. Take your frying basket and add the cauliflowers
4. Fry for 5-6 minutes, making sure to shake them halfway through
5. Once done, take the cauliflowers out and serve them
6. Enjoy!

### Nutritional Contents:

- Calories: 240.9
- Fat: 5.5g
- Carbohydrates: 6.2g
- Protein: 8.8g

## Fried Pineapple Bites

Serving: 4

Prep Time: 5 minutes

Cook Time: 15 minutes

### Ingredients:

- 3-4 pieces of Raw Banana
- 1 teaspoon of Salt
- ½ a teaspoon of Turmeric Powder
- ½ a teaspoon of Chaat Masala
- 1 teaspoon of olive oil

### Directions:

1. Cut the pineapple in half and take the skin away, remove the crowns
2. Take out the inner core cut in half again into 4 wedges
3. Pre-heat your Fryer to 352-degree Fahrenheit
4. Brush the lime juice all over the pineapple
5. Transfer the pineapple to your fryer
6. Sprinkle coconut shreds on top and cook for 12 minutes

### Nutrition Values (Per Serving)

- Calories: 467
- Fat: 12g
- Carbohydrates: 10g
- Protein: 7g

## Very "Salty" Parsnips

Serving: 2

Prep Time: 5 minutes

Cook Time: 15 minutes

### Ingredients:

- 3 Parsnips
- 2-ounce almond flour
- 1 cup water
- 2 tablespoon olive oil
- Salt as needed

### Directions:

1. Peel the parsnips and slice them up into French Fry shapes
2. Take a bowl and add water, salt, olive oil and almond flour
3. Mix well
4. Add the parsnips and coat them evenly
5. Pre-heat your Fryer to 400-degree Fahrenheit
6. Add parsnips to the fryer and cook for 15 minutes

### Nutrition Values (Per Serving)

- Calories:228
- Carbohydrate: 15g
- Protein: 4g
- Fat: 17g

## Hearty Rosemary Munchies

Serving: 6

Prep Time: 30 minutes

Cook Time: 30 minutes

### Ingredients:

- 4 medium sized russet potatoes
- 1 tablespoon of olive oil
- 2 teaspoons of finely chopped rosemary
- 2 pinches of salt

### Directions:

1. Scrub your potatoes well and wash them under water
2. Cut the potatoes into chip shapes
3. Soak the potatoes under water for about 30 minutes
4. Drain the potatoes and place them on a kitchen towel
5. Pre-heat your fryer to 330-degree Fahrenheit
6. Take a bowl and add olive oil, potatoes and mix
7. Transfer the potatoes to your fryer and cook for 30 minutes until you have a nice golden-brown texture
8. Give it a nice shake
9. Season and serve!

### Nutrition Values (Per Serving)

- Calories: 593
- Carbohydrate: 0g
- Protein: 2g
- Fat: 39g

## Fishy Calamari Bites

Serving: 5

Prep Time: 6 minutes

Cook Time: 15-30 minutes

Ingredients:

- 12-ounce frozen squid (thawed and washed)
- 1 large beaten egg
- 1 cup almond flour
- 1 teaspoons ground coriander seed
- 1 teaspoons cayenne pepper
- 1/2 teaspoons black ground pepper
- 1/2 teaspoons kosher salt
- Lemon wedges as needed
- Olive oil spray

Directions:

1. Take a large sized bowl and add flour, ground pepper, salt and paprika
2. Dredge the calamari rings in egg and then into the floured mix
3. Pre-heat your Fryer to 390-degree Fahrenheit
4. Add the rings to your fryer basket and cook for 15 minutes until they show a nice golden texture
5. Cook on batches and serve with a garnish of lemon wedge
6. Enjoy!

Nutrition Values (Per Serving)

- Calories: 227
- Carbohydrate: 8g
- Protein: 11g
- Fat: 14g

# Conclusion

Before wrapping the book, I would like to take a moment here and tell you how much I appreciate you going through the whole book.

I really do hope that you enjoyed reading this book and found it informative and helpful. Remember that with this book, you have just scratched the tip of the Ketogenic Air Frying Ice Berg. A long journey awaits ahead of you!

Be prepared and may you stay safe and healthy!

God Bless!

Made in the USA
Middletown, DE
08 August 2019